felicity Wishes

First published in 2009
by Hodder Children's Books

Felicity Wishes: Summer Album © Emma Thomson 2009
Felicity Wishes © 2000 Emma Thomson
Licensed by White Lion Publishing

Hodder Children's Books
338 Euston Road, London NW1 3BH

Hodder Children's Books Australia
Level 17/207 Kent Street, Sydney, NSW 2000

A catalogue record of this book is available from the British Library.

ISBN 978 0 340 98987 6

Printed in China

Hodder Children's Books is a division of Hachette Children's Books.
An Hachette UK Company
www.hachette.co.uk

h
Hodder
Children's
Books

A division of Hachette Children's Books

PHOTOS CAROUSEL

Felicity Wishes
Summer Album

Emma Thomson

Dear Fairy Friends,

Summer is my favourite time of the year. I enjoy going on sparkling adventures in the warm sun, discovering exciting places, and making lots of new friends, like the time I sailed across the waters of Fairy World and went backpacking to Dreamland.

This beautiful album is brimming with activities, games, stories, and a scrapbook to collect all your special memories.

Love felicity x

This Magical Book Belongs To...

Name

....

Address

....

....

Phone number

....

Birthday

....

Here's what I look like

Draw a picture or stick a photo here.

I'm on my way to

....

I'm travelling by

....

Name
................Felicity Wishes.................
Address
.....The house on top of the hill,.....
.....Little Blossoming, Fairy World.....
Phone number
.............000 111 222 333.............
Birthday
..............It's a secret!..............

Here's what I look like

I'm on
my way to
Bird Island
....
I'm travelling by
A hot-air balloon
....

Felicity is counting down the days to her summer holiday
and has drawn up a plan of her trip.

JULY

1 Go shopping.	2	3 Pack.	4	5 Hot-air balloon departs at 7am.	6 Play travel games.	7 Arrive at Bird Island and see Bea!
8 A long lie-in!	9 Catch up on the gossip!	10 Eat exotic food.	11 Go to the beach.	12 Climb Flutter Mountain.	13 Meet feathered friends!	14 Say goodbye.
15 Hot-air balloon departs at 8am.	16 Write travel journal.	17 Arrive back in Little Blossoming.	18	19	20	21
22	23	24	25	26	27	28
29	30	31				

COUNTDOWN

Where are you going and when?

August

1	2	3	4	5	6	7
8	9	10	11	12	13	14
15	16	17	18	19	20	21
22	23	24	25	26	27	28
29	30	31				

Stick your
holiday picture here.

Name
Payson

Relationship to me ....
Word that best describes this person ....

TRAVEL

ME

Name
Tyler

Name
Conrad

Relationship to me ....
Word that best describes this person ....

Relationship to me ....
Word that best describes this person ....

Name
Brandon

Relationship to me ....
Word that best describes this person ....

BUDDIES

FELICITY

Name
Polly

Relationship to me   My best friend
Word that best describes this person   Caring

Name
Holly

Relationship to me   My friend
Word that best describes this person   Fun

Name
Daisy

Relationship to me   My friend
Word that best describes this person   Thoughtful

Name
Winnie

Relationship to me   My friend
Word that best describes this person   Adventurous

Felicity always forgets to do something before she goes on holiday so she's drawn up a checklist to help her remember.

- ☑ Pack wand, crown and mobile phone.
- ☑ Buy new summer wardrobe.
- ☑ Make sure accessories coordinate.
- ☑ Pack waterproof wings.
- ☑ Pack spare pair of pink stripy tights.
- ☑ Ask Polly to help with packing.
- ☑ Have a sleepless night because I am so excited!

The most important thing Felicity takes on holiday ...Her friends...............

Felicity's most looking forward to ....Visiting her penpal.................

Whilst Felicity's away she will miss ....Sparkles Café.................

GETTING READY 3

Have you remembered everything?

- [ ] Read about the places I'm going to visit.
- [ ] Check out the places on a map.
- [ ] Find out train/bus times.
- [ ] Fill out name and address in my journal.
- [ ] Pack and then repack!
- [ ] Say goodbye to friends.
- [ ] Get really excited!

The most important thing I take on holiday ....

I'm most looking forward to ....

Whilst I'm away I will miss ....

Felicity and her friends love to play games to entertain themselves on long journeys. What's your favourite game?

Felicity Says

One player is chosen to be Felicity and tells the others to perform a series of actions: 'Put your wand on your head', 'Wiggle your wings', etc. But players must only follow the instructions when they start with the words, 'Felicity says'. Anyone who performs an action without the magic words is out of the game. Likewise, anyone who doesn't perform an action when Felicity says so is out. The last person remaining is the winner!

Fairy Friend

If you see another fairy fan, wave your wand in the air, wiggle your nose and make a wish for friendship to last forever.

Lift Your Wand, Duck Your Crown

Everyone has to raise their wands when your car crosses a bridge over water. Similarly, duck your crown when going under a tunnel.

FAIRY FUNFAIR GAME

Where in Fairy World

Someone begins the game by saying the name of a town, city or country, e.g. Little Blossoming. The next person has to say a place name beginning with the last letter of that place. In this case, it would be a place beginning with 'G', e.g. Glitter Beach. The game continues with players taking turns. If someone can't think of a place, they are out of the game. The winner is the last fairy left in the game.

Summer Sunshine

Felicity and her best friends, Holly, Polly, Daisy and Winnie, were beside themselves with excitement. Despite being squashed uncomfortably beneath enormous heavy backpacks, their fairy wings quivered with anticipation.

"I've been looking forward to this day for so long!" squealed Felicity as she landed beside her friends in the train station with a fairylike thud.

"I never thought it would actually arrive," said Winnie excitedly. "And now it has, I can hardly believe it!"

Winnie was at school with Felicity, Holly, Polly and Daisy. She wanted to be an Adventure Fairy when she graduated. It had been her idea, one lunchtime, that they all go inter-railing around Fairy World together that summer.

* * *

"Has everyone got their tickets?" asked Winnie, taking charge.

"Yes!" chorused Holly, Polly, and Daisy, waggling them in the air.

"I think so!" flapped Felicity, frantically unzipping every pocket on her rucksack. "Oh, no!" she muttered hastily under her breath.

"Um… Felicity!" said Polly, trying to get her friend's attention.

"Hold on a second," said Felicity, getting more flustered by the minute as every pocket she emptied revealed no ticket.

Polly, Holly, Daisy and Winnie stared in amazement as Felicity rummaged through the most bizarre items they had ever seen packed in a suitcase! Four bags of strawberry fizzy laces, two mobile phones (just in case she lost one and couldn't speak to her friends) and ten pairs of stripy tights!

"Felicity!" said Polly sternly, trying to get her attention. "Look!"

Felicity stopped and looked up at Polly, who was waving two tickets.

"You gave me your ticket to look after… remember!"

Felicity blushed bright pink. She always forgot things, especially when they were important.

* * *

With their tickets stamped and their bags carefully stowed away in the overhead shelves, the five fairy friends settled down for the exciting journey.

"I hope no one else joins us!" said Holly,

lounging luxuriously across the spare seat next to her.

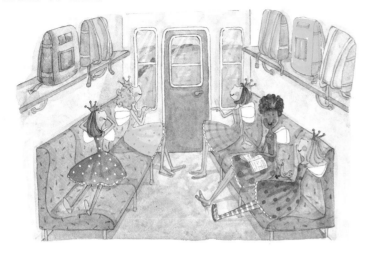

Just then the compartment door swung open.

"Hello!" said a little voice. "Is this carriage number 57?"

Holly quickly jumped up. "Um, yes, yes. Is this your seat? I was just, um, keeping it warm for you," she said as she slid over to her own seat, her cheeks a little flushed.

"Hello!" said Felicity, excited to meet a new friend. "I'm Felicity and these are my best friends, Holly, Polly, Daisy and Winnie. We're going on a backpacking holiday around Fairy World. Where are you going?"

To Felicity's amazement, the little fairy said nothing in return. Felicity watched as she started to unpack a book from her bag, kick off her shoes and curl up in her seat. It wasn't until the little fairy reached into her bag and pulled out Suzi Sparkle's latest CD that Felicity realized she was listening to a CD player and hadn't heard anything Felicity had said!

"Oh, well, there's plenty of time to make friends during the journey," thought Felicity.

* * *

As the train slowly fluttered out of Little Blossoming, the fairies left behind the billowing green hills and were soon soaring past long golden beaches, magnificent valleys and breathtaking forests.

"The view is incredible!" said Holly, mesmerized by the changing landscape.

"Just amazing," said Felicity, feeling the chug-chug of the train rocking against her tired wings.

"I'm exhausted," yawned Polly, "and we haven't even been anywhere yet!"

The excitement of the trip had drained each of the fairy friends. Ever so slowly, as every mile passed, the fairies grew sleepier and sleepier, until at last the only one who was awake was the little fairy listening to music in the corner.

* * *

"Um, hello! Hello! Wake up! Is this your stop?" said the little fairy, rustling Felicity's hair with her wand. "Hello! Yoooohoooo! If you don't wake up now I'm afraid you're going to miss your stop!" she said more loudly.

Suddenly, thinking she was in bed, Felicity rolled over and fell off her seat.

"Wha...Where am I?" she burst out,

noisily enough to wake all the others.

"It's the next stop," said the fairy. "Do you have to get off here?"

Winnie was as muddled as Felicity and had no idea how long they had all been asleep for, or where in Fairy World they were.

"Quickly, everyone!" said Winnie, taking charge. "Pack up your things; we only have a few moments to get out of here before the train leaves!"

Holly, Polly, Daisy, Felicity and Winnie flew madly about the carriage, gathering their belongings.

"My wand!" burst out Felicity. "I can't find my wand!"

"Leave it!" cried Winnie. "We have to change trains or we won't make the connection! Any moment now the train is going to pull aw—" And just as Winnie was starting to say "away", the slow roll of the train's wheels began to move underneath them.

Distraught, the five fairy friends pressed their noses up against the glass to watch in desperation as the station platform passed by.

"That platform sign says Bloomfield," said Holly, staring quizzically at the sign in the distance. "I

didn't think we had to change trains until Sweet Hill."

Everyone looked at Winnie, who looked at the tickets and then at the little fairy that had woken them up.

"You've only been asleep for half an hour. Sweet Hill is where I'm going too, but it's not for another…" and she looked at her watch, "… fourteen hours!"

Felicity, Holly, Polly and Daisy groaned, dropped their bags and slumped back into their seats.

* * *

Feeling a little better for their nap and relieved by their close escape, the fairy friends were in high spirits once more.

"My name's Felicity and these are Holly, Polly, Daisy and Winnie," said Felicity, tapping each of her fairy friends on their knee with her wand.

"And I'm Kristen," said the fairy as she took off her headphones. "I'm sorry if I seemed a little rude earlier, but I've just been given a copy of Suzi Sparkle's latest album and I was dying to listen to it."

"No, not at all," said Felicity, relieved that the fairy hadn't been ignoring them on purpose. "We all love Suzi Sparkle too."

"Why are you going to Sweet Hill?" asked

Winnie. "Are you going on holiday too?"

"Oh, no," said Kristen. "I've just had my holiday in Little Blossoming, and now I'm going home!"

"How funny," burst out Felicity. "We're almost doing the same thing, only in the opposite direction!"

"We're not staying in Sweet Hill though," said Polly. "We're just changing trains there. We're on our way to Dreamland."

"Oh, I've always wanted to go to Dreamland," said Kristen. "Absolutely anything you dream of can come true there."

"Well," said Polly, "we've got fourteen hours to go even before we get to Sweet Hill. Why don't we play some games to entertain ourselves?" she suggested, and looked around for inspiration. Suddenly she spotted an old discarded newspaper and gave each fairy a double-page sheet. "Best outfit wins!"

Polly immediately set to work making a hat. She'd learnt how to fold paper in an origami book from the library. Holly based her outfit on a pattern she had seen in the latest edition of *Fairy Girl*. Felicity and Daisy made skirts decorated with newspaper flowers and Winnie and Kristen decided to make a dress to fit both of them!

When the ticket inspector knocked on the carriage door all she could see was a sea of rustling paper pages in front of her eyes.

"Hmm, I'll come back later," she said, completely baffled.

The fairy friends couldn't control their giggles and rolled around the carriage floor in fits of laughter.

* * *

Felicity had expected the destination to be the exciting part of the journey and getting there the boring bit. But the journey was turning out to be every bit as fun.

"There's no going to sleep!" announced their new friend Kristen when she saw Holly and Polly yawn in unison. "I have to get off at 3 a.m. and you have to change then too! If we miss our stop, I'll never get home and you won't reach your holiday destination!"

So the fairy friends played games, and told silly jokes and stories late into the night.

Kristen told them all about her home, Sweet Hill. The fairy friends gasped in amazement as they tried to imagine houses that float on fluffy white clouds, a theme park where everything was edible, magical castles and, most importantly, the world-famous Sweet Hill Ice Cream Emporium.

* * *

When the train drew into Sweet Hill station the fairies had packed up their things and were busy swapping addresses and phone numbers with Kristen. They were all a little upset at saying goodbye and each made a secret wish that Kristen could come with them.

"If ever you find yourselves in Sweet Hill again, you must come and stay!" urged Kristen, who was also secretly wishing she could continue with her new friends to Dreamland. "Keep in touch!" she cried as she slowly walked away.

"Wait!" said Felicity, running after her. "You've forgotten this!" And she put the newspaper hat over Kristen's crown to remember them by.

"Right," said Winnie, getting her bearings. "Our connecting train leaves from platform five, so that should be us over there." And she pointed to a bright-red speed train with a large pair of wings on the sides of the engine.

When they reached the train, they found a ticket-inspector fairy blocking the way.

"Please accept our sincere apologies," she said, "but I'm afraid this train has broken down. The repair fairies won't be available to fix it until first thing tomorrow morning. I suggest you find something to amuse yourselves until then."

Felicity and her friends groaned.

"What are we going to do?" asked Holly, starting to panic. "It's 3 a.m. – nowhere will be open!"

"We could phone Kristen," said Felicity, suddenly perking up.

"Felicity, I think Kristen's probably climbing into her bed as we speak!" said Polly sensibly.

Felicity's heart sank. She'd been looking forward to seeing her new friend again.

"Then why don't we visit that all-night Ice Cream Emporium Kristen told us about?" said Daisy.

Suddenly Felicity perked up. She had been dreaming about super-puff berry sherbet ever since Kristen had told her about it.

* * *

The streets of Sweet Hill were magical. Morning dew settled on golden cobblestones that glittered in the lamplight. As far as the eye could see, magnificent houses floated softly on fluffy white clouds.

"I feel like I'm in a dream," said Daisy.

"I feel as though I've been here before!" said Felicity, looking around in awe. "Kristen described it all so wonderfully. It's just as I imagined."

When the fairy friends turned the next corner, Sweet Hill Ice Cream Emporium lay before them. A warm yellow light flooded out on to the street and dozens of fairies sat with ice creams that boasted more different-coloured scoops than Felicity and her friends had ever seen.

Within moments they were inside and ordering scrumptious double helpings of the weirdest and most wonderful flavours they could ever imagine.

"I'd like a scoop of super-puff berry sherbet," said Felicity excitedly to the waitress fairy behind the counter. "A friend told me it was the best."

The waitress looked awkward. "I'm very sorry," she said. "But I've just given the last scoop to that fairy over there," and she pointed in the direction of a booth in the corner.

Felicity couldn't believe her eyes. It was Kristen!

"Guess who!" said Felicity, sneaking up behind Kristen and covering her eyes. Kristen spun round and nearly fell off her stool!

"Felicity!" she cried, flinging her arms around her new friend. "What are you doing here?"

"We've come to persuade you to come with us to Dreamland!" joked Felicity.

"Oh, you don't need to persuade me!" said Kristen, laughing. "After I left you I enquired about tickets and they said that owing to a faulty train there were dozens of spare seats available on the first train tomorrow morning! There was no point in going to bed, so I thought I'd come here until it was time."

Felicity couldn't believe her ears!

"But it's our connecting train that's broken down! Now we can all go to Dreamland together!"

It was only the start of their summer adventure, but already each of the fairies' secret wishes had come true.

Summer Make and Do Fun
Pretty Postcards

♥ 1 Choose some pretty paper or card in your favourite colour.

♥ 2 Cut it into an oblong.

♥ 3 Use lovely things like photos, tickets and labels to decorate the front of your card.

♥ 4 On the back, write your letter and add the address.

♥ 5 Find a fairy postbox and send your postcard.

Tasty Treats!

On a bright summer's day, Felicity and her friends like to enjoy a special picnic lunch.

Felicity's Chunky Choc Treats

Ingredients:

350g/12oz chocolate spread

400g/14oz condensed milk

225g/8oz broken digestive biscuits

50g/2oz raisins

115g/4oz dried apricots

50g/2oz hazelnuts

Paper cake cases

Put the chocolate spread and condensed milk into a large mixing bowl. Stir together.

Add the biscuits, raisins, apricots and nuts, and mix well.

Put one generous tablespoonful of mixture in each paper case.

Put the treats in the fridge for 2 hrs while you lick the bowl and do the washing up.

♥ Make magical sandwiches by removing the crusts and using a cookie cutter to cut them into fun shapes.

♥ Decorate fairy cakes with cherries, sprinkles, chocolate flakes or sweet sugary icing.

TOP TEN TRIPS

FELICITY'S FAVOURITE PLACES

1. DREAMLAND where all your wishes come true.

2. BIRD ISLAND to see hundreds of exotic birds.

3. LAND OF SHOPPING for the best bargains!

4. SWEET HILL to visit the world famous ice cream emporium.

5. LAND OF SAND to learn the latest desert dance moves!

6. SNOW POLE to build snowfairies!

7. CAPE OF ROSES strewn with sweet-scented petals.

8. TRIFLE MOUNTAIN where everything is edible!

9. UNDERCOVER ISLAND full of secrets and surprises!

10. LITTLE BLOSSOMING my home.

...orld, but some places are very close to her heart.

MY FAVOURITE PLACES

1. ....

2. ....

3. ....

4. ....

5. ....

6. ....

7. ....

8. ....

....

9. ....

....

10. ....

....

Stick a photo here of your favourite place.

Everywhere Felicity goes, she writes a travel journal. It is a special keepsake of the magical places she has discovered. What have you seen today?

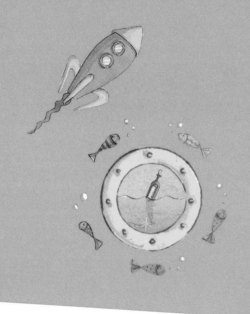

My Travel Journal

⭐ Date ....

⭐ I travelled by bus/car/coach/bike today

⭐ I ate this today ....

⭐ Today made me feel ....

⭐ Today the weather was ....

⭐ The best place I saw today

....

⭐ My favourite memory of today

....

Relax in style and have a wonderful adventure at the same time

SPARKLE BOATS

CALL US ON 788 9000

A souvenir of today

Fairy Friends

Felicity, Holly, Polly, Winnie and Daisy and their new friend Kristen were on their summer adventure, travelling around Fairy World together.

The steady rocking of their train had them nodding off within seconds. It had been a long night. The train to Dreamland had been delayed at Sweet Hill, but now they were finally on their way.

* * *

The buffet car in the train was the most glamorous the fairies had ever seen.

"Gosh!" said Holly, looking at the tables with their white linen tablecloths and silver teapots. "You don't get this on the trains in Little Blossoming!"

The fairy waitress came towards them, smiling. "We're really full, so I'm afraid you'll have to wait," she said, "unless you wouldn't mind sharing a table?"

Felicity's tummy rumbled its most enormous rumble yet.

"I think we'll share," said Holly urgently.

The fairies at the table they joined had almost finished their pudding and were huddled deep in conversation, in a language that the fairy friends had never heard before.

Felicity smiled and waved her wand in a friendly hello.

Frowning, the foreign fairies stopped talking, picked up their wands and one by one handed them over to Felicity!

"No no!" said Felicity, passing them back. "I was just saying 'hello'! I don't want your wands!"

"H-e-l-l-o," said Holly loudly.

"They're foreign, not deaf, Holly!" said Polly, laughing.

The foreign fairies got up and stood facing Felicity and her friends. Gravely they raised their left arms, spread the fingers on their right hands, placed their thumbs on their noses and in unison blew a raspberry!

"Well, how rude!" said Holly, aghast. "If they don't want us to share their table, they only have to say!"

"Is there a problem here?" said the waitress fairy, arriving just at the right

time. "I see the fairies from Dreamland have welcomed you in their traditional way."

"Traditional way?" laughed Polly, who was frantically rummaging for her phrase book.

"And it's customary," said the waitress, "to reply with a similar gesture!"

* * *

After their initial sticky start the fairies sat down to enjoy a meal together. Armed only with Polly's book they were able to discover that the Dreamland fairies were on their way home. Their names were Schubi, Blina and Lishu. At least, that's what Polly thought their names were. Felicity was of the mind that Polly might have it wrong... and that these were actually their favourite colours!

"Fancy eating your meal back to front like that!" said Holly, watching the Dreamland fairies tucking into their main course after finishing their pudding.

"I think it's very sensible," said Daisy. "If you eat your pudding first, you'll always have room for it – and puddings are the nicest bit of any meal!"

"It says here," said Polly, consulting her phrase book, "that in Dreamland anything you've ever dreamed of can happen for real!"

"What an incredible place," said Felicity, thinking of all the dreams that she'd love to come true.

"Let's ask our new friends where the best place to stay is, so that we make the most of our trip," suggested Polly. She leafed to the back of her phrase book.

"Ahem," said Polly. She cleared her throat to get the Dreamland fairies' attention. Lishu got up, clapped her hands excitedly, put her hand in her pocket and handed Polly a cough sweet.

"Ta chukka," said Polly, bemused. This isn't going to be easy, she thought. "Liff ena hise?" she said stiffly. She had no idea whether she had the pronunciation right.

USEFUL PHRASES
★ ★ ★ ★
Most commonly used phrases
Hello–Atish
How are you?–Ooooo-u
Where do you live?–
Liff ena hise?
Where can we stay? –
Ugo tta rooo men?

USEFUL PHRASES
★ ★ ★ ★
Where is the train
station?–Ugo tta
choo choo la?
Thank you–Ta chukka
Yes–Ohyi
No–Notta chonss

Lishu, Blina and Schubi beamed their biggest smiles.

"Ohyi, de en hugh gesten hise wott inde plas cool 'Daydreams'."

"What did you ask? What did she say?" said Felicity, looking expectantly at Polly.

"I asked them where they live," said Polly proudly, "but I haven't a clue what they said back!" She began frantically flicking through her book.

"I'm sure I heard her say the word 'Daydreams' at the end – that's Dreamland's capital city, isn't it?" said Daisy. "It would be perfect if that is where they're from, because that's where we're planning to visit."

"Ask them where we can stay!" urged Felicity.

Polly braced herself, smiled at the three foreign fairies and said, "Ugo tta rooo men?"

"Ohyi, ohyi," they said in unison.

"Ugo tta beein liff en wid duss forum edda," said Schubi, with nods of approval from all her friends.

"Ohyi, forum edda. Itum ma kenn ussen delli rear ee oushly hap pi," said Blina, tears welling up in her eyes.

"What was that?" said Felicity "Are you sure you asked the right question? Blina looks like she's going to cry!"

Anxious to look like she knew what was going on, Polly made a wild and almost correct guess.

"Oh, yes," she said confidently. "I asked them where we could stay and they said that the best place to stay was a hotel called 'Wid Duss' in Forum Edda."

"Forum Edda," said Felicity dreamily. "It does sound like somewhere you'd see in a dream."

"The words actually mean 'for ever'," said Polly, consulting her book. "You're right, it does sound dreamy."

* * *

For the rest of their journey the new fairy friends didn't leave the buffet car. Felicity laughed so hard that afternoon that her cheeks ached. They discovered that the best way to communicate was by drawing... but none of them was very good at it!

Holly learnt how to make a 'Dreamland wish' by closing her eyes as though she was asleep and wiggling her wand with a snore!

Kristen and Daisy bravely tried some of Lishu's biscuits. They looked like they were made of mud, but tasted delicious.

And Blina tried desperately to teach them all how to sing the Dreamland national anthem, which sounded to Felicity as if it was completely out of tune...

* * *

When Felicity, Holly, Polly, Winnie, Daisy and Kristen finally stepped on to the platform to join their new friends, they knew at once they were in Dreamland.

"Birds flying backwards!" gasped Felicity, as she pointed up to the sky.

"A café on a cloud!" squealed Polly, opening her eyes wide.

"You're never going to believe this!" said Holly. She tugged her friends to where Lishu, Schubi and Blina were standing, trying to hail a taxi.

"Self-driving bicycle taxis with wings!" said Felicity, barely able to grasp what she was seeing.

CAPE OF ROSES

TRIFLE MOUNTAIN

"I did say," said Polly, "absolutely anything you dream of can come true in Dreamland!"

"I'd like to dream that I'll stay here for ever!" said Felicity in awe.

* * *

But what was truly incredible was yet to come. As the magical bicycle taxis flew into the sky and away from Daydreams train station, the fairies didn't know where to look next.

On one side were houses shaped like lollipops with curly-wurly slides that took you to the ground. On the other was a lake, not full of water, but of fizzy yellow sherbet!

"Oh, I hope Hotel Wid Duss isn't far," said Felicity, longing to be close enough to go for a sherbet swim before they left.

"Forum Edda must be soon," said Polly. "I can feel the wheels of the bicycle beginning to dip."

"No, no," said Holly, looking down. "This isn't Hotel Wid Duss, this is their house. I recognize it from the pictures."

* * *

Schubi, Lishu and Blina lived together in a house that didn't look like anything Felicity or her friends had ever seen before. From the outside it looked like a huge beach ball, covered with windows whose shutters opened to reveal dozens of smiling fairies.

It was Polly who guessed what had happened first. When one of the fairies whisked away her backpack and she was shown to a beautiful room with everything she had ever dreamed of, her guess was confirmed.

Polly wanted to be a Tooth Fairy when she graduated from the School of Nine Wishes, and she had always dreamed of a place just perfect for her. A room with pictures of large toothy smiles on the walls, magazines about teeth and toothy tales on the bookshelf, and a duvet with a picture of her favourite front tooth.

"I don't understand," said Felicity, bursting happily into Polly's room and flinging herself on the toothy duvet. "I thought we were going to stay in Hotel Wid Duss, but I've just been shown to the most beautiful room I could ever have dreamed of. It's got pink curtains, pink carpet, pink wallpaper, pink bedclothes and even a pink light... it's pink heaven!"

Just as Polly picked up her phrase book, Kristen, Daisy, Holly, Lishu, Schubi and Blina all ran into her room.

"I'm afraid there's been a mistake," said Polly earnestly. "There is no hotel 'Wid Duss'."

"That doesn't matter!" said Holly, in ecstasy. "We can stay here! Lishu has just shown me to the most amazing room full of mirrors and make-up. There's even a

"They live with an awful lot of fairies!" said Felicity, excited at the possibility of making even more friends – with her limited drawing skills!

As the bicycles landed, all the waving fairies rushed down to the main entrance and stood to welcome them with the traditional raspberry greeting. Felicity thought she was going to pass out with giggles!

"Dis isen noo frenden," said Lishu loudly, addressing the crowd. "Holly, Polly, Felicity, Daisy, Winnie an Kristen!" she said, pointing to each of them in turn. "Dey av commen toe liff en wid duss forum edda!"

The whole throng of fairies went wild with cheers and descended on Felicity and her friends in a shower of hugs and kisses, amongst cries of, "Wid duss, forum edda!"

walk-in wardrobe full of beautiful outfits that are just my size."

Patiently Polly explained. "There is no hotel 'Wid Duss' because 'Wid Duss' actually means 'with us', and as I already said on the train, 'forum edda' isn't a place. It means 'for ever'."

Ever so slowly, what Polly was saying dawned on all the fairy friends.

"So Lishu, Schubi and Blina think that we are going to live 'with them', 'for ever'?" said Holly. She was quite keen on the idea.

Polly nodded. "Dreams only come true if you believe in them for ever, which means we will never be able to go back to Little Blossoming if we stay here for more than one night."

Felicity knew what they had to do. Dreamland was the most amazing place she'd ever seen. But Little Blossoming was their home, and she'd never be able to live anywhere else.

"How are we going to tell them we can't stay with them for ever?" said Daisy, distraught. "They've been so kind to us, and given us such a lovely place to live. Whatever we say will break their hearts!"

Suddenly, Felicity had an idea. Pulling her notebook and pen from her pocket, Felicity tried very carefully to draw the best drawing she possibly could.

When she showed Lishu, Blina and Schubi their eyes welled up with tears.

They knew that it meant their new fairy friends would not be staying for ever, as they'd hoped, but would be leaving to go home in the morning.

But before their fairy tears had rolled down their cheeks, Felicity quickly drew something on the next page that she knew the Dreamland fairies would understand.

Lishu, Blina and Schubi whooped and gave all five fairy friends one enormous hug all at the same time.

"What in Fairy World did you draw?" squealed Holly, her wings crumpling under the hug.

"I drew something that said even though we would have to go, we will never leave this place because we will always return, in our dreams… forum edda!"

And everyone cheered!

Felicity dreams of exploring new and faraway places.

If I could fly anywhere in the world I would go to

Sparkledust Island
....

My perfect travel buddy would be

Suzi Sparkle
....

When I close my eyes I dream I am

on a beach / in a city / (on a boat) / in the country
....

If I had to write a book about somewhere it would be

Land of Friends
....

If I could live anywhere in the world it would be

Fashionland
....

I would like to travel around the world to

somewhere undiscovered / (space)

Where do you go in your dreams?

If I could fly anywhere in the world I would go to

....

My perfect travel buddy would be

....

When I close my eyes I dream I am

on a beach / in a city / on a boat / in the country
....

If I had to write a book about somewhere it would be

....

If I could live anywhere in the world it would be

....

I would like to travel around the world to

somewhere undiscovered / space
....

the tilleley

I want a doylis

sophie
sophey
mum

Write down your favourite summer memories here.

Summer Memories

ones upune a time there was a litell girle colld sophey. and Hure mum was coulde sarea. sophey want a dog and cat. know i want a dad sophie showt

Explore,
Record,
Remember.

Stick your favourite fun moments on the next few pages.